# CHAMPIONS AT SPEED

28
allergies

# CHAMPIONS AT SPEED

*Written and illustrated by* RICHARD CORSON

Dodd, Mead & Company, New York

*For my sons Michael and Christopher whose education*
*included seeing some of the great ones at Watkins Glen*

Library of Congress Cataloging in Publication Data

Corson, Richard, date
    Champions at speed.

    SUMMARY: Briefly describes the racing careers of
automobile racing drivers: Tazio Nuvolari, Rudolf
Caracciola, Juan Manuel Fangio, Stirling Moss, Phil Hill,
Graham Hill, Jim Clark, and Jackie Stewart.
    1.  Automobile racing drivers—Biography—Juvenile
literature.  [1.  Automobile racing drivers]  I.  Title.
GV1032.A1C67      796.7′2′0922   [B]   [920]   78-25853
            ISBN 0-396-07656-4

# CONTENTS

# INTRODUCTION

The racing car is a thing of stunning beauty. To watch a Grand Prix driver at speed in it, absorbing its urgent signals through every nerve fiber in his body, knowing the smell of fear, is to witness the ultimate expression of man's need to measure himself against the odds. There are maybe twenty such mortals, internationally licensed, in the world at a given time. As for the rest of us, we look in awe from trackside with the mundane complaints of lesser souls: the heat, the rain, the mud. In a time when we are somehow losing our need for heroes, these men have been mine.

*Tazio Nuvolari draped with the familiar victory laurels*

# One / TAZIO NUVOLARI

The blood-red Ferrari was falling to pieces. The little two-seater had left Brescia in northern Italy before dawn, and by daylight brief glimpses of the sparkling Adriatic Sea could be seen. Toward Ravenna and Fano the racer rocketed, exhaust booming and stones flying as it took the hairpin curves broadside, in long controlled slides. Through banner-draped towns the red car charged, grazing stone walls and scattering chickens in the narrow streets.

The white-helmeted driver was climbing now, turning southwest from Fano, rocking overtaken cars in his wake. He passed some machines crumpled against rock ledges or upside down in the ravines. The Ferrari was in the spiny passes of the Apennines, and by the time the distant domes of Rome came into view the killing pace had left 150 cars behind.

North from the Eternal City it sped. Thousands of people had lined the ancient streets, their cheers unheard over the noise of the exhaust. A sudden lurch and the engine hood ripped off and sailed high over the driver's head. Through the treacherous mountain passes of Futa and Raticosa the tortured car continued to break up. The seat came loose and it was pitched over the side. The driver cushioned himself on a bag of oranges and lemons. At Leghorn, a sudden rise taken at over a hundred miles an hour snapped one spring shackle, then another. A mudguard came adrift. Officials at the Bologna checkpoint urged his retirement, but his answer was to accelerate away in a shower of gravel. Standing by the side of the road at Modena, the car's builder watched the battered wreck, and Enzo Ferrari wept.

Near Reggio the rear brakes collapsed and after several wild skids he stopped. It was four o'clock in the afternoon and a soft rain was falling over the Italian countryside. The driver sat silently in the cockpit for awhile, strangely calm. Cars screamed by, strung out now, and infrequent.

In 1930 he had won this same race (and again in 1933), when each spring between 1927 and 1957 the whole of northern Italy was transformed into a murderous race course on public roads.

It was the Mille Miglia—the Thousand Miles. (The race was banned forever after the 1957 event. Portago's Ferrari lost a wheel, killing himself, his passenger, and eleven spectators.)

After a few minutes he left the ruined car and removed the linen helmet that hid the thinning gray hair. A trickle of blood was on his chin. He went to a nearby church where a priest led him to a spare room. He slept for two hours with the grime and exhaustion of nearly a thousand hellish miles. He was a dying man, an incredible fifty-six years old, wasted by illness and personal tragedy. But for a few hours that May of 1948 he was "Il Mantovano Volante" (The Flying Mantuan) of his youth.

His name was Tazio Giorgio Nuvolari, and he was the greatest racing driver who ever lived.

Tazio was born in the little northern Italian village of Casteldario, Mantua, in 1892. He was a strange boy, undersized, moody, arrogant. Even as a lad he was a born daredevil. He climbed the tallest trees, rode the most spirited horses bareback in his father's fields. He terrorized the Mantuan countryside with the motorcycle his family bought him at fifteen. He even had a fling at flying when he patched up a Blériot monoplane that had crashed near his home, killing the pilot. Young Tazio derricked it to the roof and tied it to the chimney. Gunning the engine, he cut the rope. The flimsy plane plunged like a rock onto a haystack and burst into flames. He escaped with a damaged back and shoulder.

Nuvolari drove an ambulance in the first World War. There was a standard joke in his unit that if his passenger survived his wounds he would die of fright during the wild ride to the hospital. "You will never learn to drive an automobile," his commanding officer predicted with some inaccuracy, upon his discharge from the Italian army.

By 1920 he was racing motorcycles, and naturally became a champion. Catching sight of Tazio at the starting line whipped a crowd to frenzy. He would smile and strut, hands high over his head, his belt stuffed full of extra spark plugs and a spare drive chain draped over one shoulder. Often he wore heavy leather pads on his elbows, for he had developed the incredible knack of leaning, flat out, against walls and buildings to gain a split second.

His most remembered motorcycle race was at the Monza Grand Prix in 1928. Nuvolari was heavily bandaged, both broken legs in casts, the result of an earlier accident. He was determined to race despite his doctor's shouted warnings, but he was hoisted and tied atop his machine, looking like an Egyptian mummy. Pushed off at the start, he eventually coasted across the finishing line at a few miles an hour to be caught by his mechanics. He won, of course. He won some 300 other bike races, too, many of them secondary club events near his home.

No one has ever quite cut the figure of Tazio Nuvolari in the cockpit of a racing car. He was a small man, barely 135 pounds, five feet, five inches tall, wiry, and with an enormous jutting jaw. Ordinary racing coveralls wouldn't do for Tazio. He wore brilliant jerseys or a leather jerkin,

*At the start of a motorcycle race at Lario, Italy*

*Nuvolari in the 1934 Maserati 6C at Pescara, Italy*

blue trousers, and rundown shoes with bright yellow laces. The helmet was white linen or red leather. Often, around his neck, hung the good-luck turtle brooch presented to him by the Italian poet Gabriele D'Annunzio.

In the seat of a fiery red Alfa Romeo or Maserati he became the complete actor. He sat bolt upright, his tiny body scarcely touching the backrest. The hairy arms were straight out, moving faster than the eye could follow. He rocked from side to side, and as the situation demanded, flashed a yellow-toothed smile or a look of withering scorn. Abruptly, he would throw back his head and scream with sheer exuberance and beat the car with the palm of his hand.

Nuvolari raced in 172 major races spaced over nearly thirty years. The records show 64 wins, an incredible feat. His ability knew no bounds and even his opponents had little understanding of his breath-taking genius. Consider his trailing the unsuspecting Achille Varzi at over a hundred miles an hour *with his lights out* in the inky night of the 1930 Mille Miglia, then as the finish line approached, switched them on and swept by the astonished Varzi to win. Consider his emerging from a tunnel at the 1933 Monaco Grand Prix with his Alfa ablaze, then pushing the burning car to within 200 yards of the finish before he collapsed. Consider his beating the combined might of the Mercedes and Auto-Union cars (both financed by Hitler's Nazi Party) in the 1935 German Grand Prix, with an outclassed car and one leg in a cast.

He drove his last years coughing blood from the tuberculosis that consumed him. He tried wearing gauze masks to keep fumes from his lungs, but it was no good. They were lifting him from the car at the end.

Tazio Giorgio Nuvolari died August 11, 1953, at sixty-one, his last race only three years before. Fifty thousand people attended the funeral, and the next year they changed the route of the Mille Miglia to pass the cemetery where he slept, buried in his uniform. And where the inscription on his marble tomb read, "You will travel faster still through the heavens."

*Nearing the end of his career, the "Old Man" catnaps in the Auto-Union pits.*

# Two / RUDOLF CARACCIOLA

The Autobahn, a German superhighway, lay straight as an arrow between Frankfurt and Darmstadt. A pale crescent moon shone through the dark pines. Frost covered the concrete lanes and they gleamed white, punctuated by distant black holes that were overpass bridges. A knot of men bustled around a silvery metal monster crouched on the road, their words forming vapor echoes in the icy air.

A Mercedes touring car pulled up. Rudolf Caracciola, Germany's greatest driver, got out kissed his wife and walked toward the group. The highway was alive with German military officers, high Nazi officials and security police. Troops waited to seal off the Autobahn when the word was given. Clearly in charge was a massive greatcoated figure—Alfred Neubauer, the legendary racing team manager for Mercedes-Benz.

The object of their attention was a low, silver, sharklike car. The metal body enclosed wheels, everything, and reached almost to the road. Only a tiny Plexiglas canopy suggested the need for a driver. He would enter from the top with a special ladder and once the cover was fastened he would be sealed in an aluminum cocoon. It was a special car built only for speed records. On its nose was the three-pointed star of Mercedes-Benz. Rudi Caracciola was about to recapture the record held by Auto-Union, the other manufacturer subsidized by Nazi Germany. It was January 28, 1938.

By 8:00 A.M. the sky brightened, turning spectacular pinks and greens. A flock of birds rose out of the pine trees and wheeled toward the Taunus Mountains.

At 8:20 the frost had evaporated and the car was push-started. The Mercedes shot forward like a bullet, the enormous acceleration pinning the driver against the backrest. The road seemed to squeeze to a slender ribbon. The "black hole" overpasses came at him like missiles and he fought the tendency to duck his head. The trees on either side merged to solid walls, enclosing the measured mile like a tunnel.

It was the finish now; a fleeting glimpse of the flag. He remembered not to brake because of the thin tires. The car rolled nearly two miles before it stopped.

Turned around by the mechanics, he was off again toward the timed section. Again the illusion of the narrowing road, the terrifying overpasses, the long coast at the finish.

Neubauer was jubilant. The record again belonged to Rudi Caracciola and Mercedes (271 mph on a public road!). It was all over in half an hour. (Auto-Union's attempt to recapture the record later the same day ended in tragedy. Their car disintegrated and killed the talented Bernd Rosemeyer.)

Except for his early years and a brief spell with Italian Alfa Romeos, Rudi Caracciola drove only for Mercedes. They were unique times, for they were also the years of the Third Reich. From 1934 to the outbreak of World War II, no top German driver was to lack the finest car.

*Rudi in the powerful 1937 Mercedes W125 Grand Prix car*

Adolph Hitler saw the Fatherland's racing teams as a "measuring stick for German knowledge and German ability." There were countless publicity photographs of high Nazi officials peering into the cockpits of racing cars. Hitler even decreed a personal representative at the circuits—Korpsführer Hühnlein. He haunted the German pits, resplendent in Nazi uniform, swastikas, medals, ceremonial dagger, and binoculars.

In this odd mixture of motor racing and politics, Caracciola drove some of the most fabulous cars ever built. The 1937 Mercedes W125, for example, was a brutal car that developed 646 horsepower and could reach nearly 200 mph on open roads. Its brakes and road-holding were no match for the sheer power, and it took enormous strength to steer. Every second in it was like driving on ice, so awesome was the performance. Rudi drove it as if out for a Sunday spin. He sat low in the car, utterly relaxed. He seldom made a major mistake although he had two awful crashes from brake failure that left him nearly crippled. (A third wreck, a freakish affair, resulted from being hit in the face by a bird while practicing for the 1946 Indianapolis 500 in America.)

The direct opposite of the daring and exuberant Nuvolari, he never abused the car or over-stressed an engine. In the language of the racers he was a "soft" driver, a characteristic that made him unbeatable in the rain. His record between 1926 and 1939 is astounding; he simply won everywhere the Grand Prix cars ran.

Rudi was born at Remagen, Germany, in 1901. It was part of his personal sorrow that his disenchantment with Hitler forced him to flee to neutral Switzerland before the war. His adopted home was a beautiful villa overlooking Lake Lugano. The last years were spent in considerable pain, the legacy of his racing accidents. Rudolf Caracciola died in 1959 of a liver disease, just seven years after his last race in the cars with the three-pointed star.

*Rudolf Caracciola. They called him the*
*"Regenmeister" for his skill in the rain.*

# Three / JUAN MANUEL FANGIO

The Nürburgring—the "Ring" to fans of motorsport—is incomparable. Between 1925 and 1927 the German race course was carved from the Eifel Mountains, near the Cologne-Coblenz area. Literally, it rings the Schloss Nürburg, a ruined twelfth-century castle. For nearly fifteen miles the black road climbs and plunges through pine forests and lush meadows. There are nearly 180 curves a lap, some blind, some sweeping arcs where speeds are terrifying. Unless a driver can average ninety miles an hour through them he will never win the *Grosser Preis von Deutschland*—the Grand Prix of Germany. During race week they come to the Ring by the hundreds of thousands, to camp in the cool forests near where the fast cars will shatter the serenity. While they sleep in their tents, red deer and wild boar picnic in the garbage pits.

The course is at once uncannily beautiful, punishing, and dangerous. Stirling Moss once said he believed no more than thirty drivers in the world were capable of racing on the Nürburgring at winning speeds. (It is, alas, no longer used for the *Grosser Preis,* due to a safety movement by the drivers a few years ago. It is still used for sports car events.)

On a hot August Sunday in 1957, World Champion Juan Manuel Fangio took his place on the starting grid for the nineteenth running of the German Grand Prix. Drama was already in the air, for the "Old Man" had shattered the lap record in practice—a stunning 9 minutes 25.6 seconds. His lean, long-snouted Maserati was starting with half-full gas tanks, a move for less weight in the early stages. The strategy would require a pit stop. His major opposition would be the Ferraris of Peter Collins and Mike Hawthorn, both young Britishers. They would start with full tanks and race nonstop—if their tires held out.

By the twelfth lap the air was charged with excitement. The red Maserati swept into the pits for rear tires and fuel. Fangio was driving a spectacular race. Already he had broken his own lap record five times and led the Ferraris by half a minute. The crowd was in a frenzy as the mechan-

*Argentinian hotrod! This one was built by the young Fangio from old Ford parts.*

ics swarmed over the car. The Maserati's tail was up on the jack, gas sloshed in through a big funnel. The only spot of calm was Fangio, who had taken a leisurely drink of water and selected a new pair of goggles. The roar increased anew—the two Ferraris, nose-to-tail, screamed by into first and second place. The Maserati thumped down on its new wheels. The funnel was snatched away. The engine exploded to life and Fangio was away. He was in third position now, by 33 seconds.

But the Old Man had the bit in his teeth. He began to slash through the pine forests. Thousands waved him on from behind the fences as he slammed the car through the twisting curves and took the humpbacked bridges in airborne leaps. Astonishingly, the time behind the Ferraris lessened—32 seconds, 25, 20, 13! By the twentieth lap there was pandemonium. The loudspeakers blared. *"Achtung, achtung! Neuer runden rekord für Fangio . . . !"* He had pared his own lap record by 6 seconds. There was an unbelieving silence, then a thundering roar. The Ferraris

Juan Manuel Fangio and the Mercedes W196. On his tail is the other team car of Stirling Moss.

flashed by the pits with, incredibly, the Maserati only three seconds behind. At the Nordkehre (North Curve) Fangio took Collins' Ferrari, and near Ahremberg he passed Hawthorn and went on to win by 3.6 seconds. He had broken the lap record a total of *ten* times. At the age of forty-six, it was his virtuoso performance.

Juan Manuel Fangio was born June 24, 1911, in Balcarce, Argentina. His origins were humble and the need to help support the large family had him at work after a minimum of education. As an apprentice garage mechanic his after-hours passion was the building of hot-rods from motley heaps of old Ford and Chevrolet parts. It was the time of the *Mechanica National*—wild races across the Argentine pampas in home-built "specials." The training was excellent—if you survived.

His first race was in a stripped-down converted taxi when he was twenty-three. It fell apart at the halfway mark. Three more cars were little better, but he was learning. His breakneck style was tempered somewhat. Annoyed that a race had been halted, he was horrified to learn that five people had died in crashes. He brooded for weeks.

In 1940, fame came overnight. Fangio won the *Gran Premio International del Norte*—a grimy, dusty, and incredibly dangerous 6,000-mile race from Buenos Aires to Lima, Peru, and back. Driving a modified Chevrolet coupe, much of it over mule paths in the Andes Mountains, he was suddenly a national hero.

In Fangio's own words he was "almost fat and almost forty" when he started his career on the Grand Prix circuits of Europe. In 1949 he won six of ten starts, all minor events. By the end of the year he had earned a place on the powerful Italian Alfa Romeo team, and won his first World Championship with them in 1951. The 1952-53 seasons with a rather slow Maserati (and a bad accident at Monza, Italy) were disappointing.

In 1954, Mercedes-Benz returned to racing for the first time since World War II. Fangio headed the team, and with the brilliant young Stirling Moss in the second car, ran roughshod over the world's circuits for two years. He was Champion again in 1954 and 1955 until Mercedes retired their cars. There were Italian cars again for 1956 and 1957—Ferrari and Maserati—and the final two Championship seasons.

What kind of man was Juan Manuel Fangio? Not Hollywood's racing driver, certainly. Short, balding, plump, courtly, he looked more like the souvenir vendor than a champion driver. He sat well back in the seat cushions, relaxed as a pudding. There were no theatrics, always a calm consideration. Even in the heat of a race he was the patient teacher. Once, leading a youngster in Sweden, he kept showing him what gear he should use around the course by holding up fingers.

Fangio retired in 1958; his compassion would not let him accept the deaths of so many friends. Today he is a wealthy, revered businessman in Argentina, and certainly the best-loved man who ever drove the fast cars. He still occasionally attends the world's circuits, and when he does the hushed words spread gently around the paddock:

"The Old Man is here!"

*Fangio waves to the crowd from the streamlined version of the W196.*

# Four / STIRLING MOSS

Goodwood, the racing circuit in southern England, had always known drama. A century and a half ago fashionable folks from London journeyed down for a carefree weekend of horse racing. During World War II the Sussex farmland became Tangmere, a "satellite" airfield for the defense of London, and the sweet-scented air was slashed by the RAF Spitfire and Hurricane fighter planes. After the war a motor racing circuit was built over the old runways. It was a pleasant place, lush and beautifully planted.

At Goodwood in 1962, on Easter Monday, a preseason Formula One race was in progress. Stirling Moss was in fourth place in his Lotus when a jammed gearbox put him in the pits. Normally it would be hopeless to continue, but he began to slice back through the field and had somehow regained a lap. At St. Mary's bend, thousands were horrified to see Moss shoot straight off the course, head-on into an earth embankment. (There has been speculation that his throttle stuck wide open.) It took thirty awful minutes to cut him out of the wreck. The first official to reach him recalls the unconscious Moss struggling grotesquely as if trying to get out. Partially paralyzed and with massive head injuries, he did not regain full consciousness for a month. When he did he remembered nothing of the accident.

In May, 1963, after many, many operations and painful therapy, he went back to Goodwood where, in secret, a Lotus racing car had been prepared. Stirling had to know what remained of his uncanny talent. It had been raining but the course was beginning to dry out. He lapped the circuit for half an hour. The genius was gone. The news flashed over the wires: "I've decided to retire. I will not drive again . . ."

Stirling Crauford Moss was born September 17, 1929, the son of Aileen and Alfred Moss. His father, a dentist and farmer, had twice driven at Indianapolis. Aileen was a horsewoman and

*Stirling Moss at speed in the Rob Walker Lotus*

champion rally driver. Young Stirling and his sister Pat developed the competitive urge naturally and won equestrian events with monotonous regularity.

Moss' first motoring events, at eighteen, were in a tiny Cooper car powered with a one-cylinder motorcycle engine. He used the Cooper in a series of hill climbs—timed runs up difficult steep courses that are still popular in Europe. By 1949 he had his first taste of Continental competition, winning a Formula Three race in Zandvoort, Holland, in a bigger Cooper. Stirling's dazzling talent was spotted instantly. He drove an amazing string of races all over Europe in British cars like Kieft, H.W.M., Alta, E.R.A. All were inferior to the red cars from Italy and hardly the cars to fulfill his burning passion to win the World Driving Championship in an English machine.

By 1954 his nationalism had softened to the point of buying a private Italian Maserati 250F—which he refused to drive until two Union Jack decals were plastered to the sides. He did well enough to be invited to the Mercedes team headed by the great Fangio in 1955. The Old Man

*At Monaco in the Vanwall*

and Moss ran practically nose-to-tail all over Europe and Stirling finished the season second to Fangio in World Championship points.

Most people remember 1955, however, for his phenomenal drive in the Mercedes 300SLR sports car in the Italian Mille Miglia. With English motoring journalist Denis Jenkinson aboard as passenger-navigator, it may be the greatest race ever run. Conceding they could never memorize a thousand miles of Italian roads, they ran the course over and over in high-speed practice, smashing two cars in the process. Finally every bump, turn, bridge, piazza was noted on a roll of paper seventeen feet long and fitted in a case where it could be wound with a knob. Realizing that even shouts could not be heard over the engine and wind noise, Jenkinson worked out hand signals to let Moss crest blind hills at 170 miles an hour, for example, or enter cities at 150. It was flat-out for the thousand miles, passing even airplanes, "Jenks" vomiting from the terrible forces in the turns and losing his glasses over the side. They won in record time.

Stirling, driving for Maserati, finished second to Fangio's Ferrari again in 1956. The following year Britain finally developed a competitive Grand Prix car, the Vanwall. Moss signed eagerly. He did well for two seasons in the fast but temperamental machine, winning Formula One races in England, Italy, Argentina, Holland, Portugal, and Morocco. The coveted driving title eluded him both years, in 1958 by a single point.

Moss spent the rest of his spectacular career in private cars, Lotuses and Coopers owned by Rob Walker, the great English sportsman. There were miraculous victories at Monte Carlo in 1960 and 1961, and a classic drive at the German Nürburgring in 1961.

Stirling Moss is certainly the most famous figure in international racing even today. He continues to promote Moss the ex-driver as vigorously as he promoted Moss the driver. And who hasn't seen a third-rate movie where the country cop pulls a speeder over with the line, "Who do you think you are, Stirling Moss?"

A fitting tribute to the greatest driver who never became Champion.

# Five / PHIL HILL

Save for a magnificent twelfth-century Gothic cathedral, Le Mans, France, could be in the heart of midwestern America. It lies in a sprawl of farmland and is a major distribution center for beef, pork, wheat, and other produce. It is not the France of the travel folders. The people are industrious, frugal, and unsophisticated. They cannot understand the significance of the most famous sports car race in the world held there each June. Or for that matter why Wilbur Wright made the first European airplane flight there in August of 1908. "Old Oilcan," they called him for his ritual of circling his flimsy craft, squirting everything in sight. The townfolk didn't care much for airplanes then or fast cars now. They talk of their pigs and crops and go away during race week, leaving someone to rent their rooms to the incoming crowds.

*Les Vingt-Quatre Heures du Mans* (the Twenty-Four Hours of Le Mans) is a spectacle like nothing else in the world. The 8.3-mile course is on public roads, and except for a few kinks, is roughly rectangular. There is a long straight—the Mulsanne—(where cars in 1978 were touching 225 mph) terminated by a near-hairpin curve where a driver must brake abruptly to 30. It is not what the drivers call an "interesting" circuit. The terrain is flat and unvaried. It can be murderous, especially at night. There is often rain, and worse, patchy fog. A big Ferrari topping 200 mph might pop out of the fog, for example, and find the way blocked by a "tiddler" (a little Triumph, maybe, or an MG) traveling at half the speed. This terrifies the best of drivers.

The race starts at 4:00 P.M. on the middle Saturday of June and ends the same time on Sunday. It may attract a third of a million people from all over the world, some more interested in the huge carnival inside the course than the racing cars.

There are usually 55 entries, two drivers per car. They spell each other on schedule to prevent a repetition of the 1952 event when poor, doomed Frenchman Pierre Levegh tried to go the whole twenty-four hours alone. He almost pulled it off, too. A little over an hour from the finish, weaving like a drunken man, eyes glazed and unfocused, doubled over the steering wheel with

30

*Total exhaustion. Phil Hill after
the 1962 Monaco Grand Prix.*

stomach cramps, his engine broke. He was pulled from his Talbot incoherent and retching. He vomited for an hour, then sobbed like a baby. (Three years later his exploding Mercedes killed him and 80 spectators in motor racing's worst disaster.)

The 1958 Twenty-Four Hours was a lethal race. The Number 14 Ferrari circulated all night, sending up great sheets of spray. Pouring rain had been coming down since Saturday evening and by daybreak the red car was far in the lead. Through the watery nightmare it had been hounded by an English Jaguar, but with four hours to go the Jag finished its race in a sandbank.

At the finish a pale sun had broken through. Number 14 stopped at the pits and picked up co-driver, Belgian Olivier Gendebien, who perched on the back of the car. Together they took the victory lap past thousands of cheering people, trying not to see charred and mangled wrecks around the circuit. The driver was a remarkable American—Philip Toll Hill.

Phil was born in Miami, Florida, in 1927. In his childhood the family moved to Santa Monica, California, where his father became postmaster. California after World War II was a hotbed of sports car activity. Young Hill, always more comfortable with mechanical things than with people, eagerly joined the boom, first as a mechanic, then driving his own MG. By 1952 he began to attract so much attention in local races that he was offered sponsored drives in international events. The first, the Carrera Panamerica Mexico, was a bone-jarring, five-day, 1,900-mile event from the southern border of Mexico to Juárez, just across the Rio Grande River from El Paso, Texas. The course was little more than rocky goat trails in some places. He finished in sixth place, an astonishing performance against many of the great European drivers he had idolized.

Phil was invited to join the Ferrari team in 1956; his seven-year stay was a near-record for that often temperamental organization. He developed into one of the finest long-distance sports car racers of all time. With the Belgian, Gendebien, Hill won at Le Mans three times: 1958, 1961, and 1962.

With Formula One drives in the Ferrari single-seaters becoming more frequent, Phil found himself within striking distance of a World Championship in 1961. He was just 4 points behind

*Phil in the winning Ferrari, Le Mans, 1958*

his teammate, Wolfgang von Trips, a German Count. Tension was running high at the start of the Italian Grand Prix at Monza. Hill was leading at the end of the first lap, von Trips was third. One lap later von Trips' Ferrari shot up a bank, killing him and fifteen spectators. Philip Toll Hill went on to a bittersweet victory. America had its first World Champion, flawed only by the specter of death.

Author's note: A few days after this was written Mario Andretti became America's second World Champion. There is a tragic coincidence. As Hill's teammate von Trips was killed in the deciding race, Andretti's Championship was likewise marred by the death of Sweden's Ronnie Peterson in the team's other Lotus. Both men died in the same race—at Monza, Italy.

# Six / GRAHAM HILL

Some drivers seem to "own" certain circuits. Jimmy Clark won the Belgian Grand Prix at Spa four consecutive times, despite the fact that he detested it. Juan Manuel Fangio won three times in a row on the dangerous Nürburgring and likewise the Monza circuit in Italy. The Monaco Grand Prix at Monte Carlo belonged to Norman Graham Hill; he won it, incredibly, a total of *five* times.

In the years Graham Hill raced at Monaco the circuit was but 1.97 miles long, the tightest (and slowest) on the Grand Prix schedule. After all, the whole Principality of Monte Carlo covers only 368 acres—smaller than many industrial plants in the United States. The course threads through what must be the most glittering real estate in the world. Before recent safety changes there were all sorts of unique surprises for the errant driver: curbstones everywhere, sidewalk cafes, plush hotels, vast expanses of plate glass shop fronts, the famous gambling casino, a railroad station, a tunnel. All of these were in precarious reach of a sliding car, as was the yacht-filled harbor where Alberto Ascari's Lancia went into the Mediterranean in 1955, amid clouds of spray and hissing steam. (He survived, to die four days later in a Ferrari at Monza, Italy.) Whatever the perils of Monaco, Hill was its absolute master. He got to know His Serene Highness Prince Rainier and Princess Grace rather well, for there was always the formal ceremony at the Royal Box after each race.

If you were to ask an artist to sketch an imaginary British racing champion, the result would probably be the spitting image of Graham Hill. He looked the part. Tall, handsome, distinguished, reserved—he could have stepped from a James Bond film or the guard at Buckingham Palace.

Graham was born in London on February 15, 1929. His father was a successful stockbroker who never owned a motor car. Graham's youth, unlike many racing drivers, was spent in pristine

*Graham Hill at the U.S. Grand Prix,*
*Watkins Glen, New York*

*Graham airborne in the BRM at the Nürburgring*

cleanliness as there was no family sedan to tinker with. He had one thing in common with most drivers, however—his early schooling suffered painfully. After some technical education at Hendon, made endurable by an enthusiastic love for sports, he went on to a five-year apprenticeship with S. Smith and Sons, the famous English instrument-makers. While at Smith's he spent much of his spare time rowing with the London Rowing Club, a sport he'd become fascinated with in 1949. In 1953 (after a two-year tour with the Royal Navy) he rowed the Number 4 position in the eight-man crews at Henley. (Throughout his motor racing career his famous Oxford blue helmet was decorated with eight white oar blades.)

Hill was twenty-four years old before he learned to drive a passenger car, an old Morris 8. It was soon after that he spotted a magazine advertisement for a racing school at Brands Hatch that offered lessons at five shillings a lap. The car turned out to be a tired Formula Three Cooper. He paid for four laps and took it out. By the end of his allotted time he knew what he wanted to do with his life. He applied on the spot for an instructor's job (his experience consisted of the four laps!) and was hired. The "job" called for no salary, the rather hopeless task of maintaining the car, and a vague promise of driving a real race someday. Sure enough, in April, 1954, Graham Hill coaxed the forlorn little Cooper to the starting line—and rocketed into the lead. Eventually he finished second, with a fourth place later in the afternoon.

In August of 1954 Hill had talked himself into a job at Lotus, eventually to become one of the great racing teams. Part of his work involved being loaned to Lotus customers as a racing mechanic and sometimes as driver. The little private teams were on pitiful budgets, but they took Graham to the famous European circuits. He began to attract some notice.

In 1960 he switched to BRM. (British Racing Motors had a tormented history, starting with a brilliantly engineered 16-cylinder supercharged car that, in 1950, was really a National project. It failed miserably.) Hill did much of the testing of the new rear-engined BRMs. By 1962 the perseverance paid off—he won his first World Championship.

With Team Lotus again in 1968 he won it the second time, despite the mental anguish of teammate Jim Clark's death in Germany. The following season Graham had a terrible accident at the U.S. Grand Prix at Watkins Glen, the car somersaulting several times, smashing his legs.

His attempt at a comeback was determined but painful. Now forty, he began to think of fielding his own team. He had, in fact, been in France testing a new car. Returning to England on a foggy November day in 1975, Norman Graham Hill crashed his own plane at Elstree. Killed with him was his new young driver, the team manager, the car's designer, and both of his mechanics.

# Seven / *JIM CLARK*

A sudden silence, shattering the tempo of excitement, can be a feeling that will haunt you forever. I experienced it once when the French driver François Cevert was killed practicing for the 1973 U.S. Grand Prix at Watkins Glen. There was an eerie quiet that seemed to smother the track like a fresh snowfall. I have a friend who described it again in the hurly-burly atmosphere of a sports car race at Brands Hatch, a cozy little circuit not far from London. That tragic afternoon, too, the numbing words passed down the low line of pits: "Jim is dead . . . Jimmy Clark was killed at Hockenheim." Clark gone! Clark with the boyish smile that inspired everyone to protect him. Clark the magnificent driver who made it all look so safe. Clark gone, as an English writer put it, without ever seeing the color of his own blood. They tell of the little Scottish boy who locked himself in his room that awful day, took down the frame that held his school diploma and replaced it with a photograph of his hero.

Jim Clark was born March 4, 1936, in Kilmany, Fife, in Scotland. By the time he was six years old the family had moved to the Border country not far from England. There the Clarks settled at Edington Mains, a farm of about 1,200 acres, where they grew barley, wheat, oats, potatoes, and maintained three flocks of pedigreed sheep.

Young Jim didn't care much for school and his father removed him when he was sixteen to help with the flocks. (The "shepherd" label followed him even when he became a sophisticated jet-age World Champion.)

He was fascinated by the tractors and was as good with them as the paid farmhands. There were always plenty of cars in the Clark family that Jimmy could drive secretly out in the fields. Motor racing never occurred to him, although there was a small circuit, Winfield, only a half dozen miles from the farm. Once, coming home from a cricket match, he saw three Ecurie Ecosse (a famous Scottish racing team) C-type Jaguar sports cars running nose-to-tail on the course—a

*Jim Clark. The insignia is that of the Lotus cars he drove.*

*The perfect match: Clark and the monocoque Lotus 33*

sight that left him curiously unmoved. It was not until his sister married a man who did a bit of amateur racing that he became fascinated. Tagging along with his brother-in-law, he saw the great drivers of the day: Moss, Hawthorn, Farina, Bira; the fire in him was kindled.

Bright and early on his seventeenth birthday Jimmy applied for his driver's license at the local Taxation Office. Before long, stories began to circulate about this "nutcase called Clark" who tore around the Border country like a maniac. It soon became apparent that the "maniac" also had an unearthly talent and he began to enter nearby motoring events, rallies and time trials. A very active Scottish racing team named Border Reivers had a fast white D-type Jaguar sports car and, although Jim admitted it scared him to death, he won twelve of twenty races in 1958.

The day after Christmas, 1959, Clark drove a single-seater for the first time at Brands Hatch in Kent, England. He made such an impression on Reg Parnell, who managed the Aston Martin Grand Prix team, that he was invited to join. A few weeks later he tested the Aston at Goodwood. Not entirely by accident Colin Chapman's Team Lotus was also at the circuit and Jim tried the Formula Junior Lotus. (Formula Junior serves the same purpose in motor racing as the minor leagues do in baseball.) It was the beginning of a perfect relationship: Chapman the car designer, Clark the driver. In 1960 Jimmy shared the Formula Junior Championship with Trevor Taylor, an Englishman, both in Team Lotus 18s.

The great days of the Clark-Chapman partnership began in 1962. Chapman had developed a phenomenal car, the Grand Prix Lotus 25. It was a pencil-slim "monocoque," having a stressed-skin body like an eggshell. (In monocoque construction the aluminum outer covering carries most of the stresses on the machine instead of the conventional frame.) In the 25 the body weighed but one-sixteenth of the entire car. The weight saved was vital, of course (early racers used to drill holes in everything to save it), but Chapman went a step beyond. The frontal area was reduced dramatically by having Jimmy drive nearly flat on his back so that next to nothing stuck out in the airstream. Clark took to the skinny Lotus like a duck to water and was within one race of winning the 1962 Championship. Ridiculously, in the Grand Prix of South Africa, the oil plug fell out and the engine seized—the title was Graham Hill's in the BRM.

Jim had only to wait one year. In 1963 he put together a remarkable string of Grand Prix victories: Belgium, Holland, England, France, Italy, Mexico, and South Africa. He was only twenty-seven, the youngest Champion motorsport had known. He won his second world title in 1965.

Colin Chapman's Team Lotus increasingly became obsessed with the Indianapolis 500 and Clark nearly won it the first time out in 1963. He finished behind the American car of Parnelli Jones, who many people think should have been "black-flagged" (disqualified) for leaking oil in the final stages of the race. Jim won with surprising ease in 1965, the tiny Lotus ending the era of the big, brutal front-engined American roadsters.

On a wet, weepy spring afternoon in Hockenheim, Germany, Jimmy Clark's beautiful Lotus gave a fateful twitch and plunged off a flat-out bend into the pine trees. Speculation centered on a blown tire. He died instantly from a skull fracture. It was April 7, 1968, and he was thirty-two. A monument stands today at the spot under the rustling pines—plus a safety barrier erected, alas, too late to save the smiling Scot with the dazzling talent.

# Eight / JACKIE STEWART

The plastic glitter of Monte Carlo, a lush wooded valley of the Ardennes in Belgium, Holland's windy sand dunes, dismal flat runways of old World War II airdromes—all have echoed the thunder of Grand Prix cars. Sometimes, in past years, they have gathered at Rouen in northwestern France—Rouen, where Jeanne d'Arc was burned at the stake before Columbus found America. At the Place du Vieux-Marche where the deed was done is a restaurant dating back to 1345. Medieval Rouen seems a surprising place to find racing cars.

You cross the Seine River and go a few miles out N. 840. The big grandstand and the pits flank the narrow highway, for the circuit is on public roads. Before the gendarmes close them off you can drive the rented Renault around the same course the racers will use. At the south end of the circuit is a rough, cobblestoned, hairpin curve and you try to imagine how it felt to Fangio in the cockpit of a Grand Prix Maserati.

I first saw Jackie Stewart at Rouen in 1964. "Jock-eee Stoo-art," the French race announcer kept screaming. I had never heard of him but it soon became obvious that would change. It was a Formula Three race, a "curtain-raiser" event before the Grand Prix of France the next day. "Jock-eee" was so far in the lead, driving a little English Cooper, that it was hardly a race. Before the year ended he would turn down Formula One offers from Lotus and Cooper and sign with BRM (British Racing Motors) alongside Graham Hill.

John Young Stewart, known as Jackie, was born in Scotland on June 11, 1939. He was always around cars—his father owned a garage and prepared racing cars as part of the business. Jackie's older brother Jimmy drove for the great Scottish racing team, Ecurie Ecosse, and became quite prominent. Unfortunately, he had two horrible accidents, one at Le Mans and another at the Nürburgring; Stewart's parents were understandably reluctant to let him follow in his brother's footsteps. Instead, he turned to trap (clay pigeon) shooting and eventually won championships all

44

*Jackie Stewart, World Champion in 1969, 1971, 1973*

over Europe as a member of the British team. He had an awful shooting day qualifying for the 1960 Olympics and just missed selection.

His father's attitude about racing had softened somewhat. When Jackie was twenty-one they took a Porsche Super 90 to Oulton Park in England for him to try. The car belonged to a Glasgow racing enthusiast and was maintained by the Stewart garage. Jackie was completely hooked and went on to win many minor sports car races in 1961 and 1962 using the name "A.N. Other"; his mother was still in the dark about the budding career. She finally read of it in the local newspaper when an article on Jackie's marriage to Helen McGregor referred to his racing exploits.

Stewart broke into Formula One racing with BRM in 1965, cocky, exuberant, and eager to learn. The BRMs (Graham Hill drove the other one on the team) were no match for Team Lotus

*Stewart in the Tyrrell-Ford Formula One car*

and Jim Clark, and their best effort always seemed beset by internal politics. Even so, Jackie was third in World Championship points, an amazing feat for a rookie.

A new engine made 1966 a disastrous year for BRM, but for Stewart it helped mold his future role in motor racing—his relentless campaign for safety. On June 12, two weeks after he had nearly won the Indy 500, Jackie had a dreadful accident at Spa, a long, fast, and dangerous circuit in Belgium. In a sudden torrential thunderstorm Stewart and eight or nine other cars went off the road at better than 150 mph. Jackie was pinned in the BRM for over half an hour, drenched in gasoline that filled the monocoque body like a bathtub. The danger of fire was enormous. There were no tools to get him out—a wrench was finally borrowed from a spectator's car to remove the steering wheel. There was no fire equipment. Above the wreck was a helicopter that was assumed to be a medical team—it turned out to be a film crew for the movie *Grand Prix*. Stewart lay in a barn a long time before an ambulance arrived. It was a nightmare.

Jackie went on to win the World Championship three times—in 1969, 1971, and 1973—in French-built Matras and the Tyrrell-Fords, both campaigned by Ken Tyrrell, a gruff Englishman in the lumber business. The memory of Spa and the loss of close friends in racing accidents spurred the drive for safety. He became a thorn in the sides of racing purists. Race organizers hated to see him coming, for it often meant millions of dollars bringing a circuit up to standards acceptable to the Grand Prix Drivers' Association headed by Stewart. Mexico vanished from the schedule, as did Spa and the hallowed Nürburgring, as unsafe.

Today there are guardrails and fences where there were none. Drivers wear fireproof clothing to their eyeballs, and "spaceman" helmets pioneered by the astronauts. The car has a life-support system to provide oxygen in a fire; there are extinguishers, and titanium subframes that are enormously strong.

That is the real legacy of John Young Stewart.

## The Author / Illustrator

RICHARD CORSON's boyhood interest in race cars and aircraft has never diminished. He has attended many Grands Prix in Europe and the United States. For over fifteen years he has been on the staff of *Road & Track* magazine, writing about and drawing race cars and racing drivers. His illustrations also appear in *Flying* magazine, and his automotive artwork has been included in two annual exhibitions of the Society of Illustrators in New York City.

Mr. Corson recently retired as a junior high school teacher of math and science. He and his wife live in Watchung, New Jersey. This is his first book.